ANTONIO Gramsci died more than forty years ago, on 27 April 1937. His death was brought on by years of ill treatment in Mussolini's gaols. Yet in some ways, he has suffered more misfortune since his death from the distortion of his ideas by those who have nothing in common with his revolutionary socialist principles.

Gramsci was a professional revolutionary from 1916 until his death. Throughout this period he was insistent on the need for a revolutionary transformation of society through the overthrow of the capitalist state.

It was this that put him as a journalist on various socialist papers in the front rank of those demanding revolutionary action from the Italian Socialist Party in the fight against capitalism and war in the years 1916–18. It was this that led him to the centre of the Turin factory councils' movement in 1919 and 1920. It was this that led him to take part in the split from the reformist Socialist Party in 1921 to set up a genuinely revolutionary Communist Party. It was this that led him to take charge of that party in 1924–26. It was this, finally, that led him into Mussolini's prisons, where he tried in note form — the famous **Prison Notebooks** — to develop his own ideas about Italian society, the strategy and tactics of the struggle for state power, the building of the revolutionary party, the revolutionary press. He hoped that these notes would provide some help to others who had the same revolutionary goal as himself. Yet his writings have been seized upon by those who want to turn Marxism into an academic and *non-revolutionary* area of study.

This was initially made possible by the systematic distortion of Gramsci's ideas by the Italian Communist Party (PCI).

5

The first period of distortion

THE first period of this distortion began as soon as Gramsci died. The Stalinist leader of the PCI, Palmiro Togliatti, had the **Prison Notebooks** in his hands within weeks. He left them unpublished for ten years.

When the **Notebooks** finally began to appear in 1947, it was in a truncated, censored form. Salvatore Sechi has shown what forms the censorship of Gramsci's letters from prison took:

(1) To remove references to various Marxists — Bordiga, Trotsky, and even Rosa Luxemburg — who were being portrayed as 'fascists' by Togliatti at the time;

(2) To conceal the fact that Gramsci had broken with the Communist Party's political line in 1931;

(3) To portray Gramsci's private life as based on an idealised marriage, 'a useful myth for making people believe, on the basis of a concrete example, in Communist loyalism with respect to the unity of the nuclear family, an instrument of the collaboration with the Catholics that the Communist Party followed in the post-war period';

(4) To suppress the fact that Gramsci had tried repeatedly to get hold of books that would give him access to Trotsky's thought after his expulsion from Russia in 1929.[1]

The aim of such distortions was to present Gramsci as the loyal Stalinist *par excellence*. As such Gramsci could provide an extremely useful weapon for an ideology that inspired virtually no social thinkers of note itself — a weapon that could be used to impress other Italian intellectuals with the rich theoretical heritage of the PCI and to conceal the intellectual poverty of the Kremlin and its followers, a weapon also to use against the left, to show that the PCI, which governed Italy jointly with the Christian Democrats after 1945, was the same party that split with even the extreme left reformist Maximalists of the Socialist Party in 1921.

The censorship and distortion of his thought was necessary because Gramsci in reality did not fit the Stalinist myth. His last letter before entering prison had been a protest to Togliatti about the bureaucratic treatment given to the Left Opposition inside Russia by Stalin. Togliatti tore the letter up.[2]

In 1931 Gramsci's brother visited him in prison. Gramsci told him that he rejected the ultra-left Stalinist 'third period' policy which Togliatti was implementing. (Togliatti had expelled three central committee members for opposing the line, and, under the pseudonym

Chris Harman

GRAMSCI
versus
REFORMISM

'DURING the lifetime of great
revolutionaries the oppressing
classes constantly hounded them,
received their theories with
savage malice, the most furious
hatred and the most unscrupulous
campaigns of lies and slander.
After their death attempts are made
to convert them into harmless
icons, to canonise them, to hallow
their names . . . while at the same
time robbing the revolutionary
theory of its substance, blunting
its revolutionary edge and
vulgarising it . . . The bourgeoisie
and the opportunists within the
labour movement concur in this
doctoring . . . They omit, obscure
or distort the revolutionary side
of the theory, its revolutionary
soul. They push to the foreground
and extol what is or seems
acceptable to the bourgeoisie.'

V. I. Lenin, *The State and Revolution*

First published July 1983
This is a re-edited and updated edition of two articles
originally published in International Socialism
journal in May and June 1977.
Published by the Socialist Workers Party, PO Box
82, London E2.

ISBN 0 905998 36 7

Production by Socialists Unlimited. Printed by East
End Offset (TU all depts), London E2.

The **Socialist Workers Party** is one of a group of
socialist organisations in various countries:

AUSTRALIA: International Socialists, PO Box 46,
    Flemington, Victoria 3031.
BRITAIN: Socialist Workers Party, PO Box 82,
    London E2.
CANADA: International Socialists, PO Box 339,
    Station E, Toronto, Ontario.
IRELAND: Socialist Workers Movement, c/o 41
    Herberton Park, Rialto, Dublin 8.
UNITED STATES: International Socialist Organisa-
    tion, PO Box 18037, Cleveland, Ohio 44118.
WEST GERMANY: Sozialistische Arbeiter Gruppe,
    Wolfgangstrasse 81, D–6000 Frankfurt 1.

Ercoli, was himself in the forefront of those defending the line against Trotsky's criticisms.) Gramsci's brother was too afraid to transmit the news to Togliatti — he knew it would mean the party abandoning his brother's defence against his fascist gaolers.

Gramsci gave up his attempts to hold discussions with the other Communist prisoners because some of them, faithfully parrotting Togliatti, denounced Gramsci as a 'social-democrat' (the line at the time ruled out all collaboration with reformists because they were 'social-fascists'). One of the last political statements Gramsci made to his friends before his death expressed disbelief in the evidence against Zinoviev at the Moscow trials. Togliatti, of course, was in Moscow *applauding* the trials.[3]

After Gramsci's death Togliatti tried to present himself as his lifelong political confidant. However, although they worked together closely in 1919–20 and again in 1925–26, they were often far apart over questions of revolutionary strategy and tactics in the intervening years. And there was no contact at all between them after Gramsci's imprisonment in 1926.

The 'Eurocommunist' period of distortion

YET in the end it was Togliatti who allowed the truth about the previous distortions to come to light by releasing Gramsci's uncensored letters and notebooks for publication. In part this was because he was forced, as other old Communists began to spill the beans about what Gramsci really thought. In part this was because the passing of time made Gramsci a distant and less dangerous figure. But, above all, the aim was to inaugurate a new period in the distortion of Gramsci's ideas. The PCI was taking the first step in the break of the western communist parties from Moscow that would later be labelled 'Eurocommunism'.

In the early 1960s the PCI began to draw away from Moscow. Its leaders dreamed of being readmitted to the Italian bourgeois government from which they had been kicked out in 1947. To achieve this goal they tried to show the bourgeois parties that they were no longer dependent on the Kremlin. Togliatti, one of Stalin's chief collaborators in the 1930s, became one of his main critics after 1956.

The switch in line led to bitter disputes with the defenders of Stalin internationally and with Stalinist loyalists within the PCI itself. It was a battle on two fronts — to assert the party's independence from Stalin's heirs in the Kremlin and to prove that a government that included the PCI would not mean a drastic change in the state machine. Gramsci's previously censored criticism of Stalin became a weapon on the first front. And a distortion of Gramsci's ideas on the state was useful on the second.

Gramsci, previously the patron saint of Italian Stalinism, rapidly became the patron saint of Eurocommunism. His ideas were invoked to justify the PCI's 'historic compromise' with the Christian Democrats (the Italian Tories). In Britain he was taken up by the intellectual right wing of the British Communist Party. He was even cited to justify incomes policy![4]

Eurocommunism's star soon waned. But the interpretation of Gramsci that it fostered has lived on: spread by journals such as **Marxism Today**, in an apparently unending flow of academic books,[5] and, increasingly, as part of the common currency of the intellectual Labour left.[6]

Yet there are few Marxist thinkers whose spirit was further removed from reformism than Gramsci's. His ideas were based on notions today's reformists castigate as 'insurrectionist', 'workerist', 'spontaneist', and 'rank and filist'.

'Insurrectionism'

FROM HIS FIRST involvement in the socialist movement Gramsci had a bitter contempt for parliamentarians. He likened them in May 1918 to 'a swarm of coachman flies on hunt for a bowl of blancmange in which they get stuck and perish ingloriously'. In words that could be applied to Italy today he argued:

'The political decadence which class collaboration brings is due to the spasmodic expansion of a bourgeois party which is not satisfied with merely clinging to the state, but also makes use of the party which is antagonistic to the state [the Socialist Party].'[7]

The emphasis by Gramsci on the building of factory councils in 1919 arose from his conviction that only with new, non-parliamentary institutions could the working class carry through its revolution:

'The socialists have simply accepted the historical reality produced by capitalist initiative. They believe in the perpetuity and fundamental of the institutions of democratic state. In their view the form of these democratic institutions can be corrected, touched up here and there, but in fundamentals must be respected.

'We on the other hand remain convinced that the socialist state cannot be embodied in the institutions of the capitalist state

. . . The socialist state must be a fundamentally new creation'.[8]

Gramsci's hostility to reformism was to increase still more in the following years. This hostility was aimed not only at the right-wing social democrats around Turati but also at the extreme left social-democrats led by Serrati — the so-called Maximalists, who mouthed a terminology that would send shivers down the spines of today's Labour left. These reformists first stood back and allowed the workers of Turin to be isolated and defeated by the employers in a great strike of April 1920. Then they refused to give revolutionary leadership to the vast upsurge in militancy that produced in September 1920 the occupation of the factories throughout northern Italy. These betrayals led Gramsci to join those who split from the Socialist Party and founded the Communist Party of Italy in 1921.

Gramsci's hostility to left and right reformists alike was not a sign of 'political immaturity', which he later outgrew as many of Gramsci's current interpreters would like to pretend.[9] It remained an emphatic note in his last major effort for the Communist Party, before his imprisonment — the Theses presented to the Lyons Congress of the PCI in 1926.

The **Lyons Theses**[10] were the most mature of Gramsci's published writings. And they were directed mainly against the ultra-left Bordiga group, which had hitherto dominated the PCI. The main point of disagreement was Gramsci's insistence on exposing the reformist leaders by proposing to them united fronts on specific issues. But at the same time he was adamant that 'social democracy, although it still to a great extent conserves its social base in the proletariat, must so far as its ideology and the political function it fulfils are concerned be considered, not as a right wing of the working-class movement, but as a left wing of the bourgeoisie, and as such must be unmasked in the eyes of the masses.'[11]

This is very close to Lenin's definition of the reformist parties as 'bourgeois workers' parties'.

It is not surprising that, although they are among the best analyses Gramsci made, the **Lyons Theses** were among the last of his writings to become widely available.

Gramsci's hostility to reformism was matched by a clear understanding of the necessity of armed insurrection. As the **Lyons Theses** put it:

'The defeat of the revolutionary proletariat in this decisive period (1919–20) was due to political, organisational, tactical and strategic deficiencies of the workers' party. As a consequence of these deficiencies, the proletariat did not succeed in placing itself *at the*

9

head of the insurrection of the great majority of the population, and channelling it towards the creation of a workers' state. Instead, it was itself influenced by other social classes, which paralysed its activity.' [My emphasis.][12]

Hence the need for a Communist Party one of whose 'fundamental tasks' was 'to place before the proletariat and its allies the problem of insurrection against the bourgeois state and of the struggle for proletarian dictatorship.'[13]

Of course, there is no open mention of armed insurrection in the **Prison Notebooks**, written under the watchful eyes of fascist gaolers. But Gramsci showed in one of the few conversations he had in prison that he had not dropped his 'immature' insistence on insurrection:

'The violent conquest of power necessitates the creation by the party of the working class of an organisation of the military type, pervasively planted in every branch of the bourgeois state apparatus, and capable of wounding and inflicting grave blows on it at the decisive moment of struggle.'[14]

'Workerism'

THE key to the fight for power for Gramsci was the working class — the flesh and blood workers who toiled in the Turin factories, not the mythical, idealised workers of Stalinist and Maoist vintage. 'Capitalist concentration', he wrote in 1919, 'produces a corresponding concentration of working human masses. This is the fact that underlies all the revolutionary theses of Marxism.'[15]

This stress on the central role of the working class underlay Gramsci's involvement in the Turin factory councils in 1919 and 1920 and is to be found in the **Lyons Theses**.

'The party organisation must be constructed on the basis of production and hence of the work-place (cells). This principle is essential for the creation of a "Bolshevik" party. It depends on the fact that the party must be equipped to lead the mass movement of the working class, which is naturally unified by the development of capitalism in accordance with the process of production. By locating the organisational basis in the place of production, the party performs an act of choice of the class on which it bases itself. It proclaims that it is a class party and the party of a single class, the working class.

'All objections to the principle that bases party organisation on production derive from conceptions which are related to classes alien to the proletariat . . . and are an expression of the anti-proletarian spirit of the petty-bourgeois intellectuals, who believe they are the salt of the earth and see the workers as the material instrument of social transformation rather than as the conscious and intelligent protagonist of revolution.'[16]

The party must have intellectuals and peasants in it, but,

'it is necessary to reject vigorously, as counter-revolutionary, any conception which makes the party into a 'synthesis' of hetero-geneous elements — instead of maintaining, without any conces-sions of this kind, that it is a part of the proletariat; that the proletariat must mark it with the imprint of its own organisation; and that the proletariat must be guaranteed a leading function within the party itself.'[17]

The reason is simple — it is the working class that is the decisive revolutionary force:

'The practice of the factory movement (1919–20) has shown that only an organisation adapted to the place and system of production makes it possible to establish a contact between the upper and lower strata of the working masses (skilled workers, unskilled workers and labourers).'[18]

Gramsci was far from denying the vital importance of winning the landless agricultural labourers and peasants to the revolution. He also saw great advantage to the working class in winning over sections of the middle class. But this meant for him the working class giving a lead, not hiding its socialist aims. The revolutionaries had to be prepared to fight alongside non-revolutionaries around slogans that stopped far short of socialism, such as the demand for a more demo-cratic Constituent Assembly. But it had to be clear that:

'. . . there is no possibility of a revolution in Italy that is not the socialist revolution. In the capitalist countries, the only class which can accomplish a real, deep social transformation is the working class.'[19]

It was on this basis that, even after he had broken with Bordiga's ultra-leftism, Gramsci remained bitterly opposed to the right-wing current in the Communist Party led by Tasca (whose politics would put them way to the left of today's Eurocommunists). Gramsci insisted that it was 'pessimism' and a 'deviation' to believe that

'. . . since the proletariat cannot soon overturn the regime, the best tactic is one whose aim is, if not an actual bourgeois-proletarian bloc for the constitutional elimination of fascism, at least a passivity of the revolutionary vanguard and non-intervention of the Communist Party in the immediate political struggle, thus allowing the bourgeoisie to use the proletariat as electoral troops against fascism. This programme is expressed through the formula that the Communist Party must be the "left wing" of an opposition of all the forces conspiring to bring down the fascist regime.'[20]

The Communist Party, he said, had to put forward some of the same democratic slogans as the bourgeois opposition parties — but in order that 'these parties, thus subject to the test of deeds, will unmask themselves before the masses and lose their influence over them.'[21]

No doubt if Gramsci were alive today his would-be admirers in the PCI and the British Communist Party would insult him, as they insult the Socialist Workers Party, for not understanding the need for a 'broad democratic alliance' of 'all anti-monopoly' forces.

'Spontaneism'

THE most developed single area of Gramsci's thought concerns the fight to develop a revolutionary working-class consciousness.

He begins from the insistence that the working class cannot be trained mechanically for the struggle, like an army. Its discipline depends on its consciousness. And this in turn grows in relation to practical experience of struggle.

Gramsci's ideas on this issue grew out of a polemic against the three other main currents on the left in Italy in the first year after World War I.

The largest, led by Serrati, saw the Socialist Party as the embodiment of class consciousness. The dictatorship of the proletariat would be the 'dictatorship of the Socialist Party', as he put it. For him class consciousness was identified with the slow, methodical task of building up the party. The second current, the ultra-left revolutionaries around Bordiga, did not believe that Serrati's party would ever dare to take power. But they also saw consciousness as embodied in a party, the Communist Party, conceived as a small elite group of highly trained and disciplined cadres. Only after it had taken power for the class would soviets (workers' councils) be formed.[22] The third current, the right wing of the Communist Party led by Tasca, stressed teaching the workers on the one hand, agreements with the 'left' trade union leaders on the other. All three groups, despite their other differences, shared the notion that class consciousness was thrown down by the party leaders to the workers, like crumbs to sparrows.

For Gramsci, by contrast, the character and the lead given to the *spontaneously* developing struggles and institutions of workers determined the growth of their consciousness. For him, as for Lenin and Trotsky, the soviet was not an abstraction to be set up by the party at the right moment, but something born as an organ of workers' struggle in the factory, perhaps initially around an apparently insignificant issue — the semi-insurrectionary occupation of the factories in September 1920 was sparked off by the breakdown of union-management negotiations over the engineering national wage agreement.[23] The soviet had to develop out of an organisation that bound workers together, regardless of their craft, regardless of their union, regardless of whether they were even in unions, around the point of production, an organisation that united their struggles with those other workers linked to them in the productive process, an organisation that could express their growing awareness of their unity, strength and ability to control production.[24]

The workers' councils in Turin did not emerge out of thin air. They began life as 'internal commissions' in the factories with similar functions in many ways to those of shop stewards' committees in Britain. Gramsci saw the role of himself and his comrades on **L'Ordine Nuovo**, the paper they produced in Turin, as being to foster this spontaneous development, to generalise the internal commissions, to broaden their base, to encourage them to take over more and more powers from management, and to link up.

As Gramsci wrote:

'The problem of the development of the internal commissions became the central problem, the *idea* of **L'Ordine Nuovo**. It came to be seen as the fundamental problem of the workers' revolution; it was the problem of proletarian "liberty". For ourselves and our followers, **L'Ordine Nuovo** became the "journal of the Factory Councils". The workers loved **L'Ordine Nuovo** and why did they love it? Because in its articles they discovered part, the best part, of themselves. Because they felt its articles were pervaded by the same spirit of inner searching that they experienced: "How can we become free? How can we become ourselves?" Because its articles were not cold, intellectual structures, but sprang from our discussions with the best workers; they elaborated the actual sentiments, goals and passions of the Turin working class, that we ourselves had provoked and tested. Because its articles were virtually a "taking note" of actual events, seen as moments in a process of inner liberation ànd self-expression on the part of the working class. That is why the workers loved **L'Ordine Nuovo** and how its *idea* came to be "formed".'[25]

13

When he wrote these lines in 1920 Gramsci was still a member of the Socialist Party. It was only later in the same year, after the defeat of the occupations, that he saw the need to break with left reformism and to form a homogeneous revolutionary party. His writings on factory councils therefore lack any explicit discussion of the notion of how a revolutionary party is to work in them. But these writings do emphasise how individual revolutionaries, and the revolutionary paper, should operate to seize on the embryonic elements of communist organisation and consciousness as they emerge spontaneously, to generalise and co-ordinate them, to make workers aware of them.

Gramsci returned to the same questions in 1923, when he criticised his own willingness to bury his views for three years beneath Bordiga's dogmatism.

'We have not thought of the party as the result of a dialectical process in which the spontaneous movement of the revolutionary masses and the organisational and directive will of the centre converge, but only as something floating in the air, which develops in and for itself, and which the masses will reach when their situation is favourable and the revolutionary wave has reched its height.'[26]

Building the revolutionary party is not a matter of *inculcating* ideas into the workers through abstract propaganda. Nor is it a matter of waiting until the workers act, stirred on by the effects of economic crisis. It is a question of relating to every spontaneous, partial struggle and attempting to generalise from this. Gramsci took up exactly the same theme again expressed in the more abstract terminology of the **Prison Notebooks**, where he writes that the job of the party has to be to draw out the elements of 'theory' implicit in the collective struggles of the working class, and to counterpose this 'theory' to all the other backward, pre-existing 'theories' in the workers' heads.

'One can construct, in a specific practice, a theory which, by coinciding and identifying itself with the decisive elements of the practice itself, can accelerate the historical process which is going on, rendering the practice more homogeneous, more coherent, more efficient in all its elements, and thus, in other words, developing its potential to the maximum.'[27]

This is a far cry from the reformist vision of the Eurocommunists and some on the Labour left in Britain, who see the struggle for socialism as a slow, purely ideological process of education that leads workers to vote in ever greater numbers for the correct combination of MPs and trade union officials.

'Rank and Filism'

GRAMSCI had nothing but contempt for reformist politicians, who sought to restrict the development of the class struggle to narrow preconceived channels, 'to obstruct its clear course, arbitrarily, by pre-established syntheses'.[28] In 1919 he began to analyse the source of this obstruction, locating it in the Socialist Party parliamentarians and the trade union bureaucracy. He stressed the alienation many workers felt from their own unions and went on to analyse the origins of this phenomenon in the fact that trade unions operate to gain reforms within capitalism, and are staffed and structured accordingly.

The unions, Gramsci explained,

'are all types of proletarian organisations specific to the period of history dominated by capital . . . In this period, when individuals are valued only to the extent that they own commodities and trade their property, the workers too have become traders too in the only property they possess, their labour-power . . . They have created these enormous apparatuses for concentrating living labour, and have set prices and hours and disciplined the market. The trade union has an essentially competitive, not communist character. It cannot be the instrument for a radical renovation of society.'[29]

'Thus a veritable caste of trade union officials and journalists came into existence, with a group psychology of their own completely at odds with that of the workers.'[30]

This analysis and the experience of the Turin factory councils led Gramsci progressively to come to see the trade union bureaucracy as an active saboteur of the class struggle: 'The trade union official sees industrial legality as a permanent state of affairs. Too often he defends the same perspective as the proprietor'.[31] After the betrayal of 1920 Gramsci became fully aware of the counter-revolutionary role of the trade union leadership.

'The Turin and Piedmont general strike clashed head on with the sabotage and resistance of the trade union organisations . . . It highlighted the urgent need to combat the whole bureaucratic mechanism of the trade union organs, which form the most solid bulwark for the opportunist activities of the parliamentarists and reformists who aim to stifle every revolutionary initiative on the part of the working masses.'[32]

He could write in the **Lyons Theses** that:

'The group which leads the Confederation of Labour [the main Italian union federation in the early '20s] should also be considered from this point of view, in other words as the vehicle of a disintegrative influence of other classes upon the workers.'[33]

Nor did the Gramsci of the **Prison Notebooks** abandon these 'immature', 'workerist' and 'rank and filist' positions. He wrote in 1930:

'Neglecting, or worse still despising, so-called "spontaneous" movements, i.e. failing to give them a conscious leadership or to raise them to a higher plane by inserting them into politics, may often have extremely serious consequences.'

He related the defeat of 1920, which paved the way for Mussolini's *coup* in 1922, to the failure of Serrati, Bordiga and Tasca alike to offer such leadership to the spontaneous movements of workers and peasants:

'It is almost always the case that a "spontaneous" movement of the subaltern classes [working people] is accompanied by a reactionary movement of the right wing of the ruling class for concomitant reasons. An economic crisis, for instance, engenders on the one hand discontent among the subaltern classes and spontaneous movements, and on the other conspiracies among the reactionary groups, who take advantage of the objective weakening of the government in order to attempt *coups d'etat*. Among the most effective causes of the *coups* must be *included the failure of the responsible groups [the Socialist Party] to give any conscious leadership to the spontaneous revolts or to make them into a positive political factor.*'[34] [My emphasis.]

Of course, Gramsci was not a 'workerist', a 'spontaneist', a 'rank and filist' in the real sense of the words, in the sense of devaluing the interventionist role of Marxists in the class struggle. Quite the contrary. His own activity in 1919–20 and 1924–26 was a shining (although not, of course, perfect) example of such intervention.

The Central Argument

REFORMIST distortions of Gramsci's thought base themselves on the following argument:

Gramsci is said to show that Western societies are quite different from Tsarist Russia. The power of the ruling class in the West rests mainly, not on physical control through the military-police apparatus, but on its ideological domination exercised through a network of voluntary institutions that pervade everyday life ('civil society') — the political parties, the trade unions, the churches, the mass media. The repressive state apparatus is only one among many defences of capitalist society.

It follows that the key struggle for revolutionaries is not a direct assault on state power, but the struggle for ideological dominance, for what Gramsci calls 'hegemony'. Hegemony is won by a long drawn out process that takes many years and demands infinite patience and sacrifice on the part of the working class. In particular, the working class can only become 'counter-hegemonic' by winning over the main sections of the intellectuals and the classes they represent, because of the crucial role they play in manning the apparatus of ideological domination. The working class has to be prepared to sacrifice its own short-term economic interests in order to do this. And until it has achieved this task, has become the 'hegenomic' class, attempts to seize state power can end only in defeat. [35]

Justification for this position is claimed to rest on the distinction Gramsci makes in the **Prison Notebooks** between two types of war:
(1) War of manoeuvre, which involves rapid movement by the rival armies, with thrusts forwards and backwards as each tries to outflank the other and its cities;
(2) War of position, a long drawn out struggle in which the two armies are deadlocked in battle, each hardly able to move forward, like the trench warfare of 1914–18.

'Military experts maintain that in wars among the more industrially and socially advanced states the war of manoeuvre must be considered as reduced to more of a tactical than a strategic function . . .

'The same reduction must take place in the art and science of politics, at least in the case of the most advanced states, where "civil society" has become a very complex structure and one which is resistant to the catastrophic "incursions" of the immediate economic elements (crises, depressions, etc.).'[36]

The last successful example of war of manoeuvre applied, in other words frontal assault on the state — was the October revolution in 1917:

'It seems to me that Ilitch [Lenin] understood that change was necessary from the war of manoeuvre applied victoriously in the East in 1917, to a war of position that was the only form possible in the West.'[37]

The basis for this switch in strategy lay in the different social structures of Tsarist Russia and Western Europe:

'In Russia the State was everything, civil society was primordial and gelatinous; in the West . . . when the State trembled a sturdy structure of civil society was at once revealed. The State was only an outer ditch, behind which there stood a powerful system of fortresses and earthworks.'[38]

The formula of permanent revolution

'belongs to a historical period in which the great mass political parties and the great economic trade unions did not yet exist, and society was still, so to speak, in a state of fluidity from many points of view . . . In the period after 1870 . . . the internal and international organisational relations of the State became more complex and massive, and the Forty Eightist formula of the 'Permanent Revolution' [Marx adopted this slogan after the 1848 revolution] is expanded and transcended in political science by the formula of "civil hegemony".'[39]

Gramsci's formulations should not be accepted uncritically, as I shall show below. But first it must be made clear that they do not at all permit reformist conclusions.

In the first place, war of position is a *war*. It is not *class collaboration* of the sort pursued by the PCI today. Gramsci's contempt for the reformists who preached class collaboration did not alter one whit in prison. He compared their passivity in the face of the fascists to 'the beaver (who), pursued by trappers who want his testicles from which medicinal drugs can be extracted, to save his life tears off his own testicles.'[40] (Some of today's 'left' union leaders might well take note!)

In the second place, it is not a startling revelation to claim that revolutionary politics is devoted for much of its time to 'war of position'. After all, Lenin and Trotsky had argued at the Third Congress of the Communist International in 1921 *on the basis of the Russian Bolsheviks' experience* for united fronts with reformist parties in order to win a majority of the working class to communism. They fought bitterly against the ultra-left 'theory of the offensive' then much in vogue, particularly in the German Communist Party — the view that the Communist Parties could simply storm forward to the seizure of power, without the support of the majority of the class, through repeated insurrectionary adventures. Gramsci acknowledged Trotsky's role in turning the Comintern toward the tactic of united fronts.[41] And he explicitly identifies the 'war of position' with 'the formula of the United Front'.[42]

In the **Lyons Theses** Gramsci sought to apply the united front tactic to Italy. The adoption of this tactic (which he had previously followed Bordiga in opposing) did not represent any slackening of Gramsci's hostility towards the reformists. He wrote of 'the tactic of the united front as political activity (manoeuvre) designed to unmask so-called proletarian and revolutionary parties and groups which have a mass base.'[43] The tactic is adopted towards 'intermediate formations which the Communist Party combats as obstacles to the revolutionary preparation of the proletariat.'[44]

In the third place, the battle for hegemony is not simply an ideological battle. It is true that Gramsci continually rejects the belief that the deterioration of workers' economic conditions leads automatically to revolutionary consciousness. He stresses this point because in the **Prison Notebooks** he is concerned to refute the then current Stalinist 'third period' thesis that the world crisis on its own would lead to world revolution. He bends the stick in order to deal with this mechanistic deviation from Marxism.

But Gramsci never denies the determining role of the economy in political life. So while 'it may be ruled out that immediate economic crises of themselves produce fundamental historic events', 'they can simply create a terrain more favourable to the dissemination of certain modes of thought, and certain ways of posing and resolving questions involving the entire subsequent development of national life'.[45] He formulated the relation between the economy and ideology in these terms: 'mass ideological factors always lag behind mass economic phenomena' and so 'at certain moments, the automatic thrust due to the economic factor is slowed down, obstructed or even momentarily broken by traditional ideological elements'. It was precisely because of this lagging of ideology behind the economy that the intervention of the revolutionary party in the economic struggles of workers was necessary to win them from the reformists.

'Hence . . . there must be a conscious, planned struggle to ensure that the exigencies of the economic position of the masses, which may conflict with the traditional leadership's policies, are understood. An appropriate political initiative is always necessary to liberate the economic thrust from the dead weight of traditional policies.'[46]

And in one of the central passages of the **Prison Notebooks** Gramsci returned to the experience of the Turin factory councils movement of 1919–20 in order to contrast the convergence of Marxist theory and spontaneous workers' struggles that took place there with both narrow, sectional, 'corporatist', economic struggles and a purely intellectual and 'voluntaristic' approach that preached politics to workers from the outside:

'The Turin movement was accused simultaneously of being "spontaneist" and "voluntarist" . . . This contradictory accusation, if one analyses it, only testifies to the fact that the leadership was not "abstract"; it neither consisted in mechanically repeating scientific or theoretical formulae, nor did it confuse politics, real action, with theoretical disquisition. It applied itself to real men, formed in specific historical relations, with specific feelings, outlooks, fragmentary conceptions of the world, etc., which were the result of "spontaneous" combinations of a given situation of material production with the "fortuitous" agglomeration within it of disparate social elements. This element of "spontaneity" was not neglected and even less despised. It was *educated*, directed, purged of extraneous determinations; the aim was to bring it in line with modern theory [Marxism] — but in a living and historically effective manner. The leaders themselves spoke of the "spontaneity" of the movement, and rightly so. The assertion was a stimulus, a tonic, an element of unification in depth; above all, it denied that the movement was arbitrary, a cooked-up venture, and stressed its historical necessity. It gave the masses a "theoretical" consciousness of being creators of *historical* and institutional *values*, of being founders of a State. This unity between "spontaneity" and "conscious leadership", of "discipline" is precisely the real political action of the subaltern classes.'[47]

In the fourth place, the struggle to win over other oppressed classes (or for that matter the more backward layers of the working class) does not mean the abandonment by the working class of the fight for its own interests. When Gramsci contrasted the 'corporatist' with the 'hegemonic' approach,[48] he was contrasting those who merely defend their own interests within capitalist society, as reformist trade unionists do, with those who project their struggle as holding the key to the liberation of all oppressed groups.

In Italy in the 1920s and 1930s the hegemonic approach implied a break with the old reformists' strategy of trying to gain concessions for the workers of the North by acquiescing in the impoverishment of the landlord-and-priest-ridden South.[49] Instead the working class had, as well as fighting for improvement in its own situation, to offer land to the peasants and the prospect of a more worthwhile society to the intelligentsia.

As in the struggle for working class consciousness, the key to winning the peasantry was to be found in the linking of political questions to practical demands. Again and again, Gramsci criticises the extreme radicals (the Action Party) in the struggle to unify Italy in the nineteenth century (and by implication the reformist socialists in the 20th century) for failing to take the only *action* that would break the hold of reaction and Catholicism in the South — the fight to divide the big estates among the peasants. Because it saw the struggle for hegemony as a purely *intellectual* struggle, the Action Party missed out. 'The failure to solve the agrarian problem led to the near impossibility of solving the problem of clericalism.'[50]

The working class might have to make 'certain sacrifices of an economic-corporative kind' in order to gain the support of other classes. 'But there is also no doubt that such sacrifices and such a compromise cannot touch the essential; for though hegemony is ethical-political, it must also be economic, must necessarily be based on the decisive function exercised by the leading group [the working class] in the decisive nucleus of economic activity.'[51]

There is no indication whatsoever that Gramsci had in the **Prison Notebooks** abandoned his position in the **Lyons Theses**, according to which the workers had to go out of their way to win over the peasants, but this could only be done by building workers' committees based on the economic position of workers in the factories and using these committees to stimulate the formation of peasants' committees. Interestingly, although Gramsci spoke of 'ruling blocs' and although he stressed the need of the working class to win the peasantry, he did not use the then fashionable Stalinist jargon about 'worker-peasant blocs'. Still less did he conceive of the middle-class intellectuals as an ally on the level of equality with the working class. They could only be won to follow its lead in the course of struggle.[52]

In the fifth and final place, Gramsci *never* suggests in the **Prison Notebooks** that the struggle for hegemony can by itself solve the problem of state power. Even in a period when the 'war of position' plays a predominant part, Gramsci speaks of a ' "partial" element of movement',[53] of 'the war of manoeuvre' playing 'more a tactical than a strategic function'.[54]

To put it another way: most of the time revolutionaries are involved in ideological struggle, using the tactics of the united front in partial struggles to win leadership from the reformists. Nonetheless, there are periodic moments of violent confrontation, when one side or other tries to break through the other's trenches by frontal assault. Armed insurrection remained for Gramsci, as he made clear in his prison conversations, 'the decisive moment of struggle'.

The stress on 'war of position' in the **Prison Notebooks** must be set in its historical context. It is a metaphor designed to hammer home a concrete political point — the revolutionary will of a few thousand revolutionaries at a time of crisis does not create the preconditions for a successful insurrection. These preconditons have to be prepared by a long process of political intervention and ideological struggle. To think otherwise, as did Togliatti and other 'third period' Stalinists in the early 1930s, was sheer madness. In the circumstances, Gramsci was less concerned to argue for the necessity of armed insurrection — after all, the Stalinists were at the time hell-bent on organising armed uprisings however hopeless — but to stress, as Lenin had in July 1917, and again in the case of Germany in 1921, that an insurrection can succeed only with the active support of the majority of the working class.

It is therefore misleading to apply the metaphor as if it were of universal validity independent of its historic context. After all, even in purely military terms, static 'war of position' is not always appropriate — as the French general staff discovered to its cost when the German tanks bypassed the Maginot line in 1940.

Ambiguities in Gramsci's formulations

ANY metaphor as liable to misinterpretation as Gramsci's 'war of position', 'war of manoeuvre' distinction must itself be open to criticism. Perry Anderson has pointed out an interesting article that Gramsci's metaphors involve a number of ambiguities and contradictions, a conceptual 'slippage' capable of being used by reformists to distort the revolutionary essence of Gramsci's work.[55]

Certainly, Gramsci's contrast between 'war of manoeuvre' and 'war of position' is rather vague. At one point the transition from the political 'war of position' takes place after 1871; yet at another it is shifted to the post-stabilisation of the world capitalist economy in the early 1920s. This confusion over timing is important because it leaves unsettled whether 'war of position' is an eternal strategy or one appropriate only in certain periods. Some of Gramsci's formulations suggest the former interpretation. But it must be ruled out by his repeated insistence on the interaction between the revolutionary party and the 'spontaneous struggles' of the class, and belief in the necessity of armed insurrection.

A second confusion lies in the contrast between Russia and the West. The contrast involves a misinterpretation of the Russian revolutionary movement. In fact, the first attempts at a 'war of manoeuvre' — the armed attacks on the Tsarist regime by the Decembrists in the 1820s and the Populists who succeeded in assassinating the Tsar in 1881 — failed. Subsequent generations of revolutionaries *had to adopt a different strategy*. The overthrow of the autocracy required a prolonged 'war of position' — ten years of Marxist discussion circles and another ten years of 'economistic' agitation before the mass party could emerge in 1905, and then 12 years of recuperation of forces. This 'war of position' was necessary to prepare the ground for the 'war of manoeuvre' in 1905–06 and 1917.

To extend Gramsci's metaphor: the military war of position becomes obsolete and dangerous with the discovery of a new weapon that can break through the other side's defences, as the tank could at the end of World War I (although it was not used to real advantage) and at the beginning of World War II. The political equivalent of the tank is the sudden spontaneous revolutionary 'thrust from below' (in Gramsci's words) of the masses, that took even Lenin by surprise in February 1917. Revolutionaries cannot adapt to these sudden changes without a *rapid switch* from a defensive posture to one that relates to the new 'war of manoeuvre', attempting to guide and influence the forward surge. Lenin's greatness lay in his ability to grasp when the strategic switch from 'war of position' to 'war of manoeuvre' must be made.

What Lenin (and Trotsky and Rosa Luxemburg) grasped was that the long drawn out struggle for hegemony, for an organisation and consolidation of one's own forces, is necessary at certain stages in the history of the revolutionary movement. But it contains within it a danger — the very success of organisation at one stage in the struggle leads to conservatism when there is a shift in the mood of the masses.

After all, the archetype of the party waging the 'war of position' in pre-World War I Europe was the German Social Democratic Party (SPD). It built up a huge network of 'fortifications' within bourgeois society — hundreds of papers, hundreds of thousands of party members, local co-ops and clubs, a women's movement, a powerful trade union machine, even a theoretical journal capable of attracting admiration from some sections of established intellectuals. Its attempt to maintain these 'positions' when the World War broke out led it to move from opposition to class collaboration. (Interestingly, the very metaphor of the 'war of positions and manoeuvre' was employed in terms very close to Gramsci's by Kautsky against attacks by Rosa Luxemburg on the SPD's reformist leadership in 1912.)[56]

Russia, Italy and the West

ITALY is taken by Gramsci as the prototype of the society in which 'the war of position' is necessary. Yet Italy in the 1920s and 1930s was far from being a typical advanced capitalist society. The things Gramsci regards as characteristic of 'civil society' — the church, urban political and cultural association, the multiplicity of bourgeois and petty bourgeois parties, the influence of 'functional intellectuals' such as teachers, lawyers and priests — seem today to be a *transient* historical phenomenon, symptomatic of Italy's *backwardness* in the 1920s and 1930s, the numerical preponderance of the peasantry, the lumpenproletariat and the petty bourgeoisie. Even *urban*-based political and cultural associations tend to decline in importance in truly advanced capitalist societies.

In Britain, and the same is true of the other advanced capitalist countries, the post-war period has been characterised by the phenomenon of 'apathy' — a falling away of mass participation in political and cultural associations such as the Labour Party and the WEA, the decline in the political influence of the Orange Lodges in Liverpool and Glasgow, a halving in the number of active church members in ten years. The 'functional intellectuals' — the lawyers, teachers, priests, doctors — no longer play a key role in local opinion formation.

Advanced capitalism leads to a *centralisation* of ideological power, to the atomisation of the masses — with the crucial exception of workplace-based union organisation — and to a weakening of old political and cultural organisations.

On the one hand the intensification of the labour process has played a role — shift work makes the organisation of local political or cultural associations difficult; on the other hand, the commercialisation of social life, the advent of radio and television, and the concentration of control over the mass media, have weakened the attractiveness of other 'leisure' activities. The number of effective structures of 'civil society' between the individual and the state has fallen. More and more the means of mass communication provide a direct intermediary. At the same time, the significance of workplace-based trade union organisation has grown dramatically; to become the one institution of 'civil society' not subverted by the atomisation.

In the circumstances, the 'defensive network of trenches' available to the ruling class in a time of crisis becomes very weak indeed once workers really move into action. Indeed, the bourgeoisie becomes critically dependent upon the trade union bureaucracy, and to a lesser extent upon the reformist political organisations, to hold back the working class. But over time this leads to an erosion of faith in the reformist leaders and to spontaneous eruptions by workers that even they cannot control. Under such circumstances a real 'war of manoeuvre' can develop, in which workers, despite their lack of revolutionary consciousness, find themselves in direct conflict with the capitalist state.

As Tony Cliff pointed out in a very important article in 1968, advanced capitalism creates 'privatisation' and 'apathy'. But 'the concept of apathy is not a static one. When the path of individual reform is closed apathy can transform itself into its opposite, direct mass action. Workers who have lost their loyalty to the traditional organisations are forced into extreme, explosive struggles on their own.'[57]

Gramsci's metaphors were used 45 years ago to deal with concrete problems of strategy. Those who now claim to be his followers attempt to deploy them in a crude way to block off discussion today, without noticing that in the years since society has changed in certain crucial ways. That is a piece of dogmatism no different to the treatment Marx, Lenin or Trotsky have suffered on so many occasions.

Gramsci's weaknesses

The conditions in which Gramsci lived and wrote imposed certain built-in limitations to his thought. In the case of the **Prison Notebooks** these limitations provide the basis for the distortions to which his ideas have been subjected.

The first and most obvious limitation was that the fascist state was looking over Gramsci's shoulder, reading every word he wrote. To avoid the prison censorship he had to be vague when referring to some of the most pointed concepts of Marxism. He had to use an ambiguous Aesopian language that concealed his real thoughts, not only from his gaolers, but also often from his Marxist readers and sometimes, one suspects, from himself.

To take a crucial point, Gramsci often uses the bourgeois struggle for power against feudalism as a metaphor for the workers' struggle for power against capitalism. But the comparison is dangerously misleading. Because capitalist relations of production have as their starting point commodity production, the production of goods for the market, which can develop within feudal society, the bourgeoisie can use their growing economic dominance to build up their ideological position *within* the framework of feudalism before seizing power. However, the working class can become economically dominant only through taking collective control of the means of production, which requires the armed seizure of political power. It is only then that they will gain control of the printing presses, universities, and so on, where the capitalists were able to buy these up long before becoming politically dominant. Gramsci necessarily had to seem ambiguous on this point. But today the ambiguity provides an excuse for would-be intellectuals who want to pretend they are fighting the class truggle through 'a theoretical practice', 'a struggle for intellectual hegemony', when in fact they are only advancing their own academic careers.

Moreover, Gramsci could not write openly about armed insurrection. This gap in the **Prison Notebooks** has enabled his claimed followers to ignore the harsh reality of the state power that held Gramsci in its grip.

But there were other, non-physical limitations on Gramsci. He went to gaol just as Stalin was tightening his hold on Russia. His failure to come to terms with this process marked his thought more deeply than may at first be apparent.

Gramsci declared his support for the Stalin-Bukharin bloc formed in 1925. He seems to have accepted as part of an international 'war of position' the attempt to build 'socialism in one country' through making concessions to the peasants. So he identified Trotsky's opposition to socialism in one country with an ultra-left rejection of the united front — even though he knew perfectly well that Trotsky was one of the main authors of the tactic of the united front.

Gramsci, as we have seen, was very aware and very critical of the suffocating bureaucratism of Stalinism. But his acceptance of the Bukharin-Stalin version (1925–28) of 'socialism in one country' prevented him analysing what had gone wrong in Russia. He writes, in the **Prison Notebooks**, 'The war of position demands enormous sacrifices by infinite masses of people. So an unprecedented concentration of hegemony is necessary, and hence a more 'interventionist' government which will take the offensive against the oppositionists . . .'[58]

Yet this half-apology for totalitarian trends is followed by a warning quotation from Marx: 'A resistance too long prolonged in a besieged camp is demoralising in itself. It implies suffering, fatigue, loss of rest, illness and continual pressure, not of the acute danger which tempers, but of the chronic danger which destroys'.

Gramsci seems to want to both criticise this state of affairs, and to say that it is based upon a correct strategy. This contradiction cannot fail to have debilitating effects on other aspects of his theory.

In 1919–20 he grasped as no-one else in Western Europe the interrelation of the struggle in the factory and the creation of the elements of a workers' state. He also came to see the dialectical interplay between the development of workers' democracy and its propellant, the revolutionary party. This understanding remains in much of the work **Prison Notebooks** — but at points it is corroded by the tendency to see the Stalinist 'socialism in one country' as providing a method for waging the 'war of positions' to be copied elsewhere.

Gramsci was not unique in failing to come to terms with Stalinism. At the time he was imprisoned and lost contact with the international movement the full horrors of Stalinism were a thing of the future. Future prominent Trotskyists as varied as Andreas Nin and James P Cannon still supported Stalin against Trotsky at that time. But in Gramsci's case the failing left an element of confusion in his theory that is seized on by those trying to justify reformist policies today.

There is one final more fundamental weakness in Gramsci. Although he provides a correct *abstract* account of the relation between economics and politics, Gramsci is alone among the great Marxists in not integrating a *concrete* economic dimension into his political writings. This produces an arbitrariness in his writings that does not exist in Marx, Engels, Lenin, Luxemburg or Trotsky. For instance in 1925 he thought fascism was about to collapse. Yet in the **Prison Notebooks**, a few years later, he wrote as if it faced a long life. Again, he talks of the dangers of a 'corporate' integration of the working class into the system, without discussing the economic conditions that could make this possible.

In general, there is a failure to show the real interrelation between a particular economic situation and political and ideological struggles of individuals it affects. In the years 1918–26 he was able to fill this gap to some extent by relying on his direct experience of the class struggle. So his best writings are those where, mixing with the workers and trying to guide them, he is grappling with central problems of current struggles.

But in 1926 the fascist state snatched him away from any contact with the masses. Gramsci was only too aware of what this meant:

'Books and magazines contain generalised notions and only sketch the course of events in the world as best they can: they never let you have an immediate direct, animated sense of the lives of Tom, Dick and Harry. If you are not able to understand real individuals, you are not able to understand what is universal and general.'[59]

This was true of Gramsci, who was unable, without direct personal experience, to grasp the concrete interrelation between the economic situation and the political reaction to it of individuals. But it was not true, say, of the Marx who from exile could write the **18th Brumaire,** or the Trotsky who from confinement in Turkey could write profoundly about daily developments in Berlin.

The **Prison Notebooks** suffer above all from this inability to move from abstract concepts to concrete analyses of concrete situations. It is this, of course, that appeals to those bureaucrats and academics who want a reformist 'Marxism' divorced from the mass struggles of workers.

If such a project runs counter to the main thrust of Gramsci's life and thought, we should not ignore the weakness in the **Notebooks** that arises from their lack of concreteness. Whatever their insights they do not have the greatness of the finest works of Marx, Lenin or Trotsky.

The fascist prosecutor at Gramsci's trial demanded his imprisonment 'to stop this brain working for 20 years'. The fascists did not succeed in this attempt. But, by cutting Gramsci off from direct involvement in the class struggle, they did succeed in preventing his Marxism from fully realising the potential displayed in **L'Ordine Nuovo** and the **Lyons Theses**.

Notes

1. **Spunti Critici sulle 'Lettere dal Carcere' di Gramsci.**
2. A. Davidson, **Antonio Gramsci** (London 1977) page 240.
3. Davidson, page 269.
4. See the speech by David Purdy at the Gramsci Conference, Polytechnic of Central London, 6 March 1977.
5. One recent representative but particularly grotesque example of which is Roger Simon, **Gramsci's Political Thought** (London 1982).
6. See for example the speech by Stuart Holland MP to the 1980 'Debate of the Decade' in **The Crisis and Future of the Left** (London 1980) page 21.
7. A Gramsci, **Selections from the Political Writings 1910–20** (hereafter referred to as **PW 1910–20**) (London 1977) page 43.
8. **PW 1910–20**, page 76.
9. See, for example, Betty Matthews' review of **PW 1910–20** in the **Morning Star**, 3 March 1977.
10. The **Lyons Theses** are translated in full in A Gramsci, **Selections from Political Writings 1921–26** (hereafter referred to as **PW 1921–26**) (London 1978) pages 340–375.
11. **PW 1921–26**, page 359.
12. **PW 1921–26**, page 349.
13. **PW 1921–26**, page 357.
14. Report of a conversation with Gramsci by Athos Lisa, **Rinascita**.
15. **PW 1910–20**, page 93.
16. **PW 1921–26**, page 362.
17. **PW 1921–26**, page 363.
18. **PW 1921–26**, page 363.
19. **PW 1921–26**, page 343.
20. **PW 1921–26**, page 359.

21. **PW 1921–26**, page 375.
22. See the articles by Bordiga in **PW 1910–20**.
23. See P Spriano, **The Occupation of the Factories** (London 1975).
24. See especially **PW 1910–20** section II.
25. **PW 1910–20**, pages 293–4.
26. Quoted in Davidson, page 208.
27. A Gramsci **Selections from the Prison Notebooks** (hereafter referred to as **PN**) (London 1971) page 365.
28. **PW 1910–20**, page 46.
29. **PW 1910–20**, page 99.
30. **PW 1910–20**, page 105.
31. **PW 1910–20**, page 268.
32. **PW 1910–20**, page 320.
33. **PW 1921–26**, page 355.
34. **PN**, page 199. Gramsci illustrates his argument with an example from medieval Italian history, but clearly he has in mind the defeat of the factory occupations and the rise of fascism. See also **PN**, page 225.
35. For examples of this argument see Roger Simon, **Gramsci's Political Thought**, and 'Gramsci's Concept of Hegemony', **Marxism Today**, March 1977.
36. **PN**, page 235.
37. **PN**, page 237.
38. **PN**, page 238.
39. **PN**, page 243.
40. **PN**, page 223.
41. See **PN**, page 236 — although Gramsci, for reasons of his own to which we will return, elsewhere identifies Trotsky with the 'theory of the offensive'.
42. **PN**, page 237.
43. **PW 1921–26**, page 373.
44. **PW 1921–26**, page 373.
45. **PN**, page 184.
46. **PN**, page 168.
47. **PN**, page 198.
48. Gramsci did not, however, invent this terminology, as many Gramsci 'scholars' who have neglected to study the history of the Comintern think. See, for instance, G Zinoviev, 'The NEP Peasant Policy is Valid Universally' in H Gruber (ed.) **Soviet Russia Masters the Comintern** (New York 1974).
49. See Gramsci's article on 'Some Aspects of the Southern Question' in **PW 1921–26**, pages 441–62.
50. **PN**, page 101.
51. **PN**, page 161.
52. Phrases about such 'blocs' have been attributed to him as part of the fashionable 'Gramscian' phraseology. But they *hardly ever* appear in his own writing and when the word 'bloc' is used it is usually in quotation marks and applies to bourgeois coalitions of forces.
53. **PN**, page 243.
54. **PN**, page 243.
55. P Anderson, 'The Antimonies of Antonio Gramsci', **New Left Review** issue 100. The article is even more interesting because it knocks down so many positions defended by Anderson himself in the past.
56. Anderson, pages 61–9. See also L Basso, **Rosa Luxemburg** (London 1975) pages 152–3 note 148.
57. T Cliff, 'On perspectives' in **International Socialism** issue 36, page 16. Reprinted in T Cliff, **Neither Washington nor Moscow** (London 1982) page 234.
58. **PN**, pages 238–9.
59. Letter to Tatiana, November 1928, quoted in C Boggs, **Gramsci's Marxism** (London 1977) page 62.

Other publications from the SWP